La Corda d'Oro

5

Story & Art by Yuki Kure

Characters

Kahoko Hino
(General Education School, 2nd year)

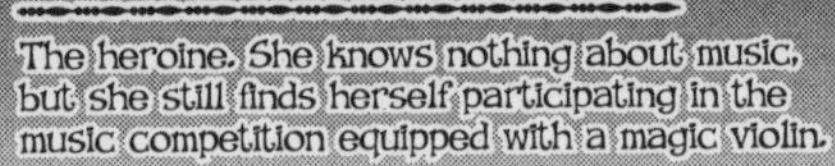

The heroine. She knows nothing about music, but she still finds herself participating in the music competition equipped with a magic violin.

Len Tsukimori
(Music School, 2nd year)

A violin major and a cold perfectionist from a musical family of unquestionable talent.

Ryotaro Tsuchiura
(General Education, 2nd year)

A member of the soccer team who seems to be looking after Kahoko as a fellow Gen Ed student.

Keiichi Shimizu
(Music school, 1st year)

A student of the cello who walks to the beat of his own drum and is often lost in the world of music. He is also often asleep.

Kazuki Hihara
(Music school, 3rd year)

An energetic and friendly trumpet major and a fan of anything fun.

Azuma Yunoki
(Music school, 3rd year)

A flute major and the son of a graceful and kind traditional flower arrangement master. He even has a dedicated fan club called the "Yunoki Guard."

Hiroto Kanazawa
(Music teacher)

The contest coordinator whose lazy demeanor suggests he is avoiding any hassle.

Story

Our story is set at Seiso Academy, which is split into the General Education School and the Music School. Kahoko, a Gen Ed student, encounters a music fairy named Lili, who gives her a magic violin that anyone can play. Suddenly, Kahoko finds herself in the school's music competition, with good-looking, quirky Music School students as her fellow contestants! Kahoko comes to accept her daunting task and finds herself enjoying music. However, the road ahead is rocky, as Len refuses to accept her and Azuma shows a dark side that only Kahoko seems to see...

Previously ...

With the Second Selection right around the corner, it's suddenly announced that Len's parents, both renowned musicians, will be attending. All eyes are on Len, and some students hold a grudge against his apparently perfect life. Every time Kahoko feels like she's connected with Len, they seem to butt heads, but the moment of truth is about to arrive on the competition stage!

The music fairy Lili, who got Kahoko caught up in this affair. ↓

La Corda d'Oro

CONTENTS
Volume 5

Measure 19 5

Measure 20 37

Measure 21 69

Measure 22 83

Measure 23 114

Special Edition—Tempo Primo 148

Backstage
with the Journalism Club 181

End Notes 188

La Corda d'Oro
MEASURE 19

AAAH...
Welcome!
PLEASE, MR. AND MRS. TSUKIMORI, WE HAVE SEATS FOR YOU OVER HERE.
SEISO ACADEMY
Whoa!
MR. TSUKIMORI'S PRETTY HOT HIMSELF!
Does Len take after his mother?
OOH
LOOK! IT'S MISA HAMAI!
OMG!
WOW! SHE'S AS PRETTY AS HER PICTURES!
OOH
WISH I COULD SIT CLOSER!
AAH

Daily Happenings ⑪

...DVDs, continued

I wrote in volume 4 that I often watch DVDs while I work. I'm not sure if that's why, but I find myself buying them a lot these days (though not an incredible amount).

But my choices aren't anything that's come out recently (almost all of them are promotional DVDs). I get all the stuff I used to be into when I was still in school.

They just take me back...

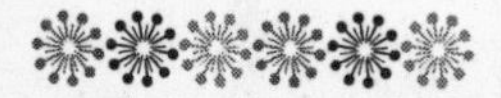

D-does this mean I'm getting old? Sigh...
A slight shock to the system...

THE WEIRDEST PART WAS...
SORRY TO COME AT SUCH A SHORT NOTICE, LEN.
BUT WE'RE LOOKING FORWARD TO THIS. WE HAVEN'T SEEN YOU PERFORM IN A WHILE.
I'M NOT SURE IF I CAN MEET YOUR EXPECTATIONS, BUT I'LL GIVE IT MY BEST EFFORT.
YOU THINK LEN TALKS LIKE THAT TO HIS PARENTS ALL THE TIME?
Figures, I guess...
HIS MOTHER'S MISA HAMAI... Right?
She's so pretty.
SHE'S THE REAL THING.
Right on.
WE TRULY APPRECIATE EVERYTHING YOU'VE DONE FOR LEN...
...AND YOUR INVITATION TODAY.
OH, NO. WE'RE ABSOLUTELY HONORED TO HAVE YOU HERE.
ER...

IT'S RYOTARO, ISN'T IT?
AS A FELLOW PIANIST, I LOOK FORWARD TO YOUR PERFORMANCE.
SMILE
Y...
BLUUUUSH
YOU'RE WAY TOO KIND!
PTU
WHO KNEW RYOTARO WAS SUCH A BIG FAN OF LEN'S MOTHER?
I HAD NO IDEA YOU GOT STARSTRUCK BY CELEBRITIES.
TEE HEE HEE
Never would've thought.
SHUT UP!
It's not like that!
WE WILL NOW BEGIN THE SECOND SELECTION OF THE SEISO ACADEMY SCHOOL MUSIC CONTEST.
THE FIRST PERFORMER IS RYOTARO TSUCHIURA, FROM THE GENERAL EDUCATION SCHOOL, SECOND YEAR, CLASS 5...
Eep...
YIPE
HEY, NOW...
...WHAT'RE YOU GETTING NERVOUS FOR?
PULL YOURSELF TOGETHER.
NOK

...PERFORMING CHOPIN'S FANTASIE-IMPROMPTU.
CLAP CLAP CLAP CLAP CLAP
YOU'D BETTER CALM DOWN BEFORE I GET BACK.
Geez.
HE'S NOT NERVOUS AT ALL!
As if!
OH, REALLY?
SO THE PERFORMANCES GO FROM LAST TO FIRST, HUH?
AS THE FIRST RUNNER-UP, RYOTARO GETS TO DEBUT.
You guys are so cute.♡
WHUP
HUH?
......
......
Y...
Uh-huh...
YOU SCARED ME!
And what's with the heart?
WHY ARE YOU HERE?
CHECK IT OUT.
I'm staff, man.
Journalism Club
BACKSTAGE IS WHERE ALL THE GOOD STUFF GOES DOWN.
STUPID KANAYAN DRAGGED HIS FEET ABOUT GIVING ME PERMISSION.
What a lazy jerk.
SOUNDS LIKE YOU'VE GOT YOUR HANDS FULL...
I know!
Looks like he's about to start!
I KNOW LEN'S THE CENTER OF ATTENTION THIS TIME...
...BUT A LOT OF PEOPLE ARE JUST AS CURIOUS ABOUT RYOTARO. LAST TIME, HE JUST HOPPED ONSTAGE AND PLAYED LIKE A VIRTUOSO. PEOPLE WANT TO KNOW WHAT'S UP.

REALLY
?

HEY...

IN FACT ...
... SINCE THE LAST TIME I HEARD HIM...
...HE'S GOTTEN A LOT BETTER.
HE'S... PRETTY GOOD, HUH?
YEAH.
HE'S NOT CUTTING US MUSIC SCHOOL STUDENTS ANY SLACK.
TEE HEE
JUST KID-DING.
MANAMI!
OF COURSE I AM! I HAVE TO GO ON RIGHT AFTER THAT!
MA-NAMI?
WHAT'S WRONG, KAHOKO? YOU NERVOUS?
Oh.
THIS IS MANAMI MORI, MY ACCOM-PANIST.
Mr. Kanazawa introduced me.
I see.
Hi.
NICE TO MEET YOU. I'M A SECOND YEAR PIANO MAJOR.
I'M NAMI FROM THE JOURNAL-ISM CLUB.
Nice to meet you, too.

WAAAA
...SECOND YEAR, GENERAL EDUCATION SCHOOL, CLASS 2... KAHOKO HINO...
B-DMP
IT'S ME...
CLAP CLAP CLAP CLAP CLAP CLAP CLAP
HE'S GOOD!
Such a light touch...
SIGH
I THOUGHT HE WAS ON THE SOCCER TEAM!
He looks like a jock, but his music's so refined!
...NEXT, OUR SECOND PERFORMER...
B-DMP
B-DMP
CLAP CLAP CLAP
BRR... HOW CAN I CALM MY NERVES?
MY HANDS ARE ALL SWEATY AND MY LEGS ARE SHAKING...

COME ON! FORGET IT!
SNAP
...PLAYING KREISLER'S JOY OF LOVE.
GOOD LUCK.
THANKS.
CLAP CLAP CLAP CLAP CLAP
THAT'S RIGHT. I DECIDED TO GIVE IT MY ALL.
I'VE DECIDED NOT TO THINK ABOUT...
Ready when you are.
...MAGIC VIOLINS AND BEING A NOVICE AND ALL THAT STUFF.
CLAP CLAP CLAP

I DON'T KNOW IF...
...THAT MAKES ME A LIAR OR A FAKE.

SHE LOOKS PRETTY CALM.
YEAH, AT LEAST COMPARED TO THE FIRST SELECTION.
...
ALL I CAN DO IS...
...BELIEVE IN...

... THIS VIOLIN AND MYSELF.
WAAAAA
CLAP
CLAP
CLAP
CLAP
CLAP
CLAP
CLAP
CLAP
CLAP
CLAP
CLAP
CLAP
CLAP

THE GEN ED DUO'S NOT BAD.
YEAH, THEY'RE PRETTY SOLID.
GOOD JOB, KAHOKO!
It was great!
It's true.
OH, PLEASE.
I was so nervous.
AAH
Kaho's awesome!
Her hard work paid off.
ESPECIALLY RYOTARO! WHAT'S HE DOING IN GEN ED?
WHEW. I'M SO GLAD IT'S OVER.
Yeah, really.
BUT KAHOKO'S IMPROVED, TOO.
She's way more confident.
AAH
AAH
OUR THIRD PERFORMER IS KAZUKI HIHARA, A THIRD-YEAR MUSIC SCHOOL STUDENT FROM CLASS B...
BUT MY HEART'S STILL RACING...
I was nervous, too! Was the pace all right?

...PLAYING MENDELS-SOHN'S ON WINGS OF SONG.
ALL RIGHT!
SLAP
KANAYAN! A PROMISE IS A PROMISE!
I got it! I got it!
GET OUT THERE, ALREADY.
SCRAM!
CLAP CLAP CLAP
PROMISE?
DON'T ASK...

THUMP
KAZUKI JUST STARTED.
I SHOULD PROBABLY GET BACK BEFORE SHOKO GOES ON.

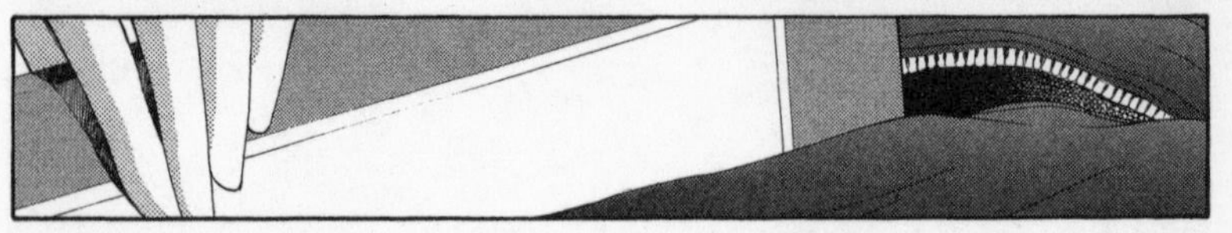

SIGH

ZIP
TUP
JUST PLAY LIKE YOU ALWAYS DO.
SHOVE
!

SL
AM
!!

WAA
CLAP CLAP CLAP
CLAP CLAP CLAP
CRAP! HE'S ACTUALLY DOING WELL!
Huh?
IS THAT A PROB-LEM?
I PROMISED THAT IF HE PLACED IN THE TOP THREE, I'D TREAT HIM TO AN ALL-YOU-CAN-EAT MEAL...
YOU'RE BRIBING HIM WITH FOOD?
It just happened.
THE KID EATS LIKE A HORSE.
Great... No savings this month.
SERVES YOU RIGHT.
NEXT... FROM THE MUSIC SCHOOL, FIRST YEAR, CLASS B... SHOKO FUYUUMI...
...PLAYING ROMANCE BY SAINT-SAENS.
C'MON, SHOKO! IT'S UP TO YOU TO TAKE DOWN KAZUKI!
MR. KANA-ZAWA!
Um...
...?!
YOU THINK PRESSURING HER'S GONNA HELP?
I WAS JUST KIDDING.
Don't get so mad.

HE'S HOPE-LESS.
...
LEN?
HEY...
...LEN'S NOT AROUND, IS HE?
I haven't seen him.
HEY.
I SAW HIM STEP OUT A WHILE AGO.
He's probably in the waiting room.
WAITING ROOM?
IS IT BECAUSE YOU'RE NERVOUS ABOUT YOUR PARENTS COMING?
IT'S NONE OF YOUR BUSINESS.
Um...
DID HE SEEM... WEIRD TO YOU?
I MEANT TO TALK TO HIM ABOUT IT, BUT I HAVEN'T HAD THE OPPORTUNITY ...
I DON'T THINK SO. WHY? IS SOMETHING WRONG?

Long time no see! Hello! Yuki Kure here.

My sincerest thanks for picking up Volume 5 of *La Corda*. ♪

Since the covers for Volumes 3 and 4 were of the second and third-year students, I decided to go with the first-years for this one. It was sort of a refreshing experience.

Well, I hope you enjoy this volume.

MAYBE THE BATH-ROOM?
WAAA
YOU ALL RIGHT, SHOKO? YOU LOOK PALE....
CLAP CLAP CLAP CLAP
sigh
Geez.
IT'S BECAUSE YOU SCARED HER BEFORE HER PERFORMANCE.
You okay, Shoko?
MY BAD.
But you did well.
HEY, KANAYAN. ISN'T LEN BACK YET?
Kinda pushing it, isn't he?

YEAH.
IT'S LEN, SO I'M SURE HE'S FINE, BUT...
3: Kazuki Hih
4: Shoko F
5: Keiichi Shimizu
6: Azuma Yunoki
7: Len Tsukimo
I'LL GO LOOK AROUND.
I'LL HELP YOU!
THANKS. I OWE YOU GUYS.
...WHICH MEANS...
...IT'D REALLY HELP IF YOU COULD WALK SLOWLY AND TAKE UP AS MUCH TIME AS POSSIBLE WHILE YOU'RE ONSTAGE!
THANKS.
OKAY... I'LL DO MY BEST...
TUP
...MUSIC SCHOOL, FIRST YEAR, CLASS A... KEIICHI SHIMIZU...
...PLAYING SAINT-SAENS'S *THE SWAN*.
...

SO...
...WHERE SHOULD WE START?
Hmm...
KAHOKO CHECKED OUT THE WAITING ROOM, RIGHT?
SHOULD WE GO THERE FIRST?
GOOD IDEA.
I JUST CAN'T IMAGINE WHERE HE'D GO.
EXCUSE ME...

HE'S NOT BACK YET!
WHERE'D YOU GO, LEN?
HEY!
RYOTARO! KAZUKI!
WHAT'RE THEY DOING?
HEY HEY
DA!

I CAN'T FIND HIM!
OUT-SIDE?
I'LL GO, TOO...
YEAH, RIGHT. IN THOSE SHOES?
OH, GOOD. WE WERE JUST COMING TO GET YOU.
BUT IT'S ALMOST HIS TURN!
NO KIDDING. SO WE'LL LOOK FOR HIM.
KAHOKO!
A COUPLE OF MUSIC SCHOOL STUDENTS SAID THEY SAW HIM GO OUTSIDE.
ER...
GEEZ!
THEN I'LL MAKE SURE HE'S NOT INSIDE!
GREAT.

WHERE'D YOU GO, LEN?

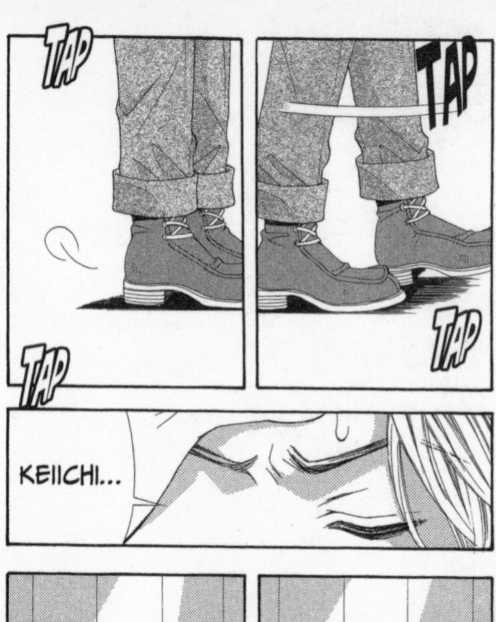
TAP
TAP
TAP
TAP
KEIICHI...

TAP

HEH
HA HA
HEE
HEE HEE

TAP
TAP
TAP
TAP
TAP
TAP
TAP
TAP

Slowly... walk slowly...
I WORRY ABOUT HIM.
Maybe it's a sign of inner strength.

WHAT? KEIICHI'S ALREADY ONSTAGE?
Un-believ-able!
WHY WOULD HE GO OUTSIDE?
HE LEFT HIS VIOLIN AND EVERY-THING!
STOP
...
LEN LEFT HIS VIOLIN?
...MUSIC SCHOOL STUDENTS SAID THEY SAW HIM GO OUT-SIDE...
...MUSIC SCHOOL?

WAIT!
WAAAAA
CLAP CLAP CLAP CLAP CLAP CLAP CLAP
NO WAY ...
THOSE GUYS...
...from the other day!
HUH?
IT COULDN'T BE...
TUP
...!

LEN!!
END OF MEASURE 19

For whatever reason, the screentone on the right, the one that looks like someone punched a bunch of holes in it, is called...

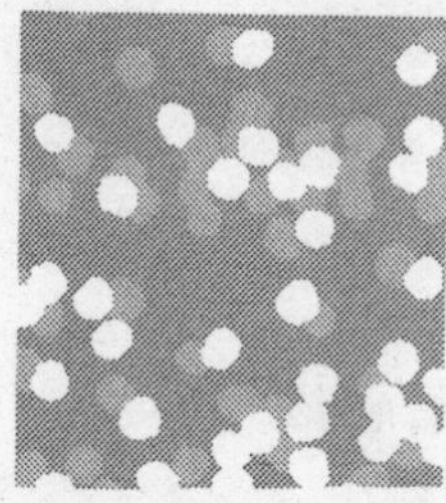

"The Azuma Screen Tone"

...around here... I don't know when it happened, but it's true that it's often used behind Azuma. I always have some handy. (lol)

La Corda d'Oro
MEASURE 20

WHERE THE HELL IS LEN? YOU KNOW HE'S NEXT!
ER, YES...
I'LL GO LOOK FOR HIM!
GREAT! NOW WE'VE LOST HIS ACCOM-PANIST, TOO!
DAMN IT!

GIVE ME A BREAK, LEN!
SLAM
...
IT'S LOCKED!
AZUMA'S ALREADY STARTED.
GRP
WHO DID THIS?
WHO WOULD ...
TWITCH
WAAA
CLAP CLAP CLAP CLAP CLAP CLAP CLAP
I GUESS I CAN THINK OF A FEW...

WAAA
CLAP CLAP CLAP CLAP CLAP CLAP CLAP CLAP CLAP CLAP CLAP
WHAT DO YOU MEAN, LEN'S NOT HERE?
YOU SEE...

KANAYAN!!
KAZUKI! DID YOU FIND HIM?
NO. SOMEONE SAW HIM GO OUTSIDE, SO ME AND RYOTARO WENT LOOKING ...
OUT-SIDE?
IS RYOTARO STILL OUT THERE?
YEAH. AND KAHOKO'S LOOKING IN THE HALLS.
I GUESS HE WASN'T IN THE WAITING ROOM...
ARE YOU SERIOUS?
I'M GONNA LOOK AGAIN!
HUH? HEY!
DAKKA DAK
...NO.
I'M VERY SORRY.
COULD YOU WAIT A LITTLE LONGER?
I'm sure he'll be back shortly...

SHUF
THERE'S NO WAY I'M GOING TO MAKE IT NOW...

NOBODY'S GOING TO COME INTO THE WAITING ROOM UNLESS THEY'RE LOOKING FOR ME.

LOOKING?

WHO'D DO THAT?
IT'D JUST MEAN MORE COMPE-TITION.
IT'D BE IDIOTIC...

WHAT KIND OF PERSON WOULD DO THAT?
...
WHAT A SIGHT FOR THEM TO BEHOLD.
Gulp

I WONDER WHEN...
KRIEEK
LEN!

...
HE'S STILL NOT BACK!
TURN
WHERE'D YOU GO, LEN?

AHH
WHERE'S THE NEXT PERFORMER?
ISN'T IT LEN? HE'S THE LAST ONE, RIGHT?
DON'T YOU THINK HE'S TAKING TOO LONG?

DARN IT! WHERE THE HECK DID HE GO?
HE'LL GET DISQUALIFIED OR HAVE TO FORFEIT.
YOU SURE ABOUT THIS? WE DIDN'T HAVE TO LOCK...
SHUT UP! YOU BACKING OUT NOW?
SEISO ACADEMY SCHOOL MUSIC CONTEST
WHAT'S GOING TO HAPPEN?
WHAT'S UP?
THANKS FOR THE TIP EARLIER.
OOPS

WE CAN'T SEEM TO FIND LEN.
FUNNY, HUH? WE'VE BEEN LOOKING FOREVER.
MAYBE HE GOT SCARED AND RAN OFF?
I BET HE WAS UNDER A LOT OF PRESSURE...
RUN OFF? WE'RE TALKING ABOUT LEN HERE.
IT'S NONE OF OUR BUSINESS ANYWAY.
SEE YOU LATER.
SL
AM
NOT SO FAST.
YOU KNOW WHAT I THINK?
I THINK YOU *KNOW* SOMETHING.

MUTTER
MUTTER
YOU REALLY THINK...
...SOMEONE THAT PROUD WOULD JUST RUN OFF?

YOU STILL CAN'T FIND LEN?
HIS PARENTS ARE HERE, YOU KNOW!

PERHAPS WE SHOULD ANNOUNCE IT ON THE PA SYSTEM.
The hall's getting restless...
SIGH
YOU'RE RIGHT ...
EXCUSE ME.
WE CAN'T KEEP EVERYONE WAITING.
IF IT'S US YOU'RE WORRIED ABOUT, PLEASE DON'T TROUBLE YOURSELF.

TWO

Measures 19 and 20 are about the Second Selection. There's a lot of Len again, continued from Volume 4. I'm using music from the *La Corda* game for their performances. Everyone besides Kahoko and Len, that is... I really love Len's piece. It's music that reminds me of him. Perhaps that's not the case for his fellow violinist, Kahoko... (lol) I also really enjoy *On Wings of Song*. I even used it again in Measure 22.

Hey...
WHY IS IT LOCKED?
HOLD ON! I'M GOING TO FIND MR. KANAZAWA AND GET A KEY!
DON'T BOTHER...
HUH?
LEN?
IT'S TOO LATE NOW.
ANYWAY, IT ONLY MEANS ONE LESS RIVAL. IT'S LIKE A DREAM COME TRUE FOR YOU.
HUH?
YOU CREEP!
YOU REALLY THINK OF US THAT WAY?

SLAM
WHAT DOES IT MATTER?
IT DOES!
NO POINT?
THERE'S NO POINT TO PLAYING NOW.
I...I WAS LOOKING FORWARD TO YOUR PERFORMANCE.
I ALWAYS THINK... IT MUST BE SO MUCH *FUN* TO BE ABLE TO PLAY THAT WELL.
AND YET...
...YOU SAY THERE'S NO POINT TO PLAYING...

I DON'T WANT TO HEAR YOU SAY THAT!
... PULL ...

I'M GOING TO PUSH FROM THIS SIDE, SO PULL.
OKAY!
KANA-YAN!
NO...
RYO-TARO!
WHY DID YOU LET EVERY-ONE LEAVE?
HOLD YOUR HORSES. THERE'S A REASON ...
KREEK

HFF
HFF
LEN!!
WHERE THE HELL HAVE YOU BEEN?
SIGH...
WHAT'S GOING ON?

IT'S LEN'S TURN!
WHY IS EVERYONE LEAVING?
WHY...
SHF
KAHOKO ...STOP.

I'M SORRY ABOUT THE TROUBLE I CAUSED.

LISTEN! IT'S NOT LEN'S FAULT!
I KNOW, I KNOW.
BUT YOU'VE GOT TO LET IT GO.
IF I'D NOTICED EARLIER...
HOW...
NO...I SHOULD'VE RUN TO GET SOMEONE AS SOON AS I FOUND HIM...
I WASN'T THINKING STRAIGHT...
IT'S NOT YOUR FAULT. DON'T WORRY.
BUT...
PAT
THE COMPETITION ISN'T OVER YET. THIS IS ONLY THE BEGINNING.
C'MON.
FLIK
OW!
EVERY-ONE'S GONE HOME ALREADY.
YOU SHOULD HEAD HOME, TOO.

NO POINT TO PLAY-ING...

IT JUST LEAVES A BITTER TASTE IN MY MOUTH.
SIGH

MRS. TSUKI-MORI.
THANK YOU SO MUCH FOR COMING TODAY.
OH, HELLO.
NO, THANK YOU FOR SHARING YOUR PERFOR-MANCE.

KAHOKO, RIGHT?

YOU HAVE SUCH A PURE SOUND. I ENJOYED IT VERY MUCH.
TH-THANK YOU SO MUCH!
I'm honored.
ARE YOU LOOKING FOR LEN?
YES, ACTUALLY.
DO YOU KNOW WHERE HE WENT?
HEY!
IT'S COMING FROM THE HALL...

IT'S AS IF...

...HE'S BEEN CAPTURED IN TIME.

EVERY-THING'S FOCUSED ON HIM...

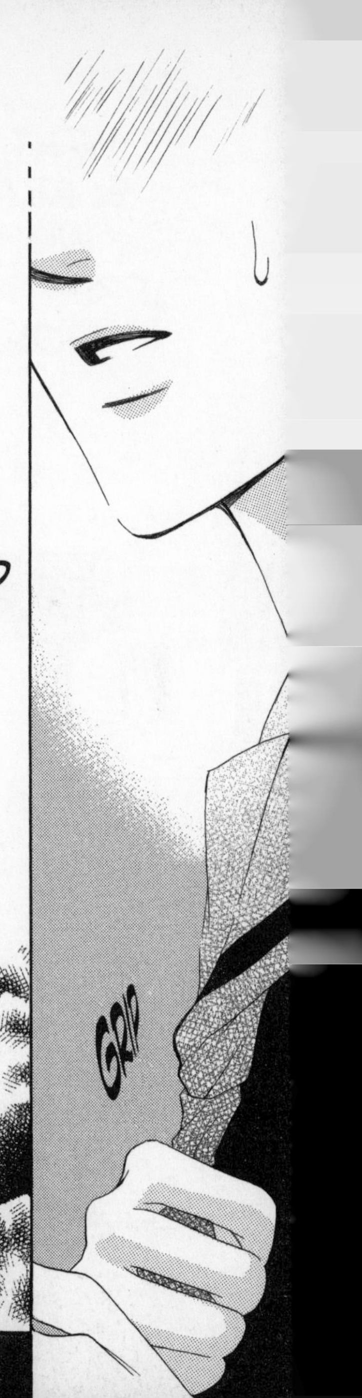
GRIP

THIS SOUND ...

WHEN DID HE...

IT'S *SCHERZO TARENTELLA* BY WIENIAWSKI. HE'S PLAYING SO BEAUTIFULLY.
HE FOCUSES TOO MUCH ON CONTESTS AND THINGS.
ALL HE NEEDS TO DO IS TO PLAY WITHOUT INHIBITION. HE CAN BE SO STUBBORN.

!
HE'S SO GOOD IT'S LIKE A SLAP IN THE FACE.
I WANT TO SCREAM WITH FRUSTRATION.

AND A VOICE IN MY HEART YELLS... "DO NOT RUN FROM THIS."

END OF MEASURE 20

La Corda d'Oro
WOOOSH
KEIICHI! YOUR ALARM WENT OFF AGES AGO!
KEIICHI!!
Daily Happenings 13
...Rubi
I realize this is out of the blue, but Shinobu's name is my favorite out of all the La Corda characters. That is, I like the kanji.
One day I got a phone call from my editor saying...
Miss Kure! Miss Kure! You won't believe it...
We typeset Shinobu's name, and the rubi...
E
Rubi?
The rubi...
俺は…
This
Type-setting
It's the rubi. Right?
14
Continued in

KEIICHI! GET UP!!
This happens every day! I'm getting sick of it!
RIP
C'MON. I'M GOING TO FOLD THE FUTON.
YOU WANT BREAKFAST, DON'T YOU?
BREAK... FAST...
La Corda d'Oro
MEASURE 21

HEE HEE
YOUR HAIR IS ALWAYS INCREDIBLE.
I GUESS THAT'S WHAT YOU GET WHEN YOU HAVE A COWLICK AND NATURALLY CURLY HAIR.
HEH
FWOOM
YES, PLEASE...
THAT'S RIGHT, KEIICHI.
YOUR SIST... TOMOMI CALLED LAST NIGHT.
I DIDN'T WANT TO WAKE YOU...
BUT REMEMBER THAT OUTFIT SHE SENT YOU FOR THE COMPETITION?
SHE WANTED TO KNOW IF YOU LIKED IT.
Don't worry. I sent her the pictures from when you tried it on here. ♪
...
THE COMPETITION...
THAT'S RIGHT. TOMOMI SENT ME SO MANY...

OH...
GOOD MORNING...
Okay, okay.
GOOD MORNING, KEIICHI. ♡
DEEP BOW.
TOMOMI'S WORRIED ABOUT YOU.
SHP
HAVING HER 15-YEAR-OLD BROTHER LIVING WITH RELATIVES AWAY FROM HOME.
WORRIED?
I DON'T THINK SHE'S CAPABLE OF SOMETHING SO COMMENDABLE.
Ha ha ha...
I don't think that's true...
SHE SAID SHE WANTED YOU TO WEAR THAT FRILLED BLOUSE.
Whew.
SHE SOUNDED DISAPPOINTED WHEN I TOLD HER YOU WORE THE ONE WITH THE TALL COLLAR.
HUH?

FRILLED?
Dear Keiichi,
I made some clothes for the contest.
I think I may have made too many,
so please choose the one you like best.
Will you take a picture and send it
to me? Pretty please?
Good luck at the contest!
FRILLED... FRILLED...

THAT LOOKS GREAT ON YOU, TOO, KEIICHI!!
Oh, my!
You look like a prince!
You should go with that!
ARE YOU SURE RELATIVES CAN'T GO TO THE COMPETITION?
IT'S SO THOUGHTLESS OF THEM TO LET ONLY THE FOLKS AT SCHOOL GO.
My goodness.
SNAP
SNAP
Smile!
...
OH... FRILLS.
THAT'S RIGHT. THE SLEEVES GOT IN THE WAY...
THEY WERE IN THE WAY...
KEIICHI!
KEIICHI! YOU'LL BE LATE FOR SCHOOL!
I KNOW YOU'RE TIRED FROM THE COMPETITION...
But you can't be late.
WHAT?
COMPETITION?
ZZZZ

Music Competition
Second Selection
First Place: Ryotaro Tsuchiura
Second Place: Kahoko Hino
Third Place: Kazuki Hihara
Fourth Place: Azuma Yunoki
Fifth Place: Keiichi Shimizu
Sixth Place: Shoko Fuyuumi
Seventh Place: Len Tsukimori
Wings of Son
Meditation
The Swan
Romance
Scherzo Tarente
THAT'S RIGHT... THE RESULTS WERE POSTED YESTERDAY...
ARE YOU SERIOUS? THE TOP TWO ARE FROM GEN ED?
WHAT'S THE MUSIC SCHOOL DOING?
And where was Len?
I HEARD RUMORS THAT IT'S A REALLY CLOSE RACE...
YEAH...
Ryotaro for real, man.
Wow.
THE FIRST YEARS REALLY BLEW IT.
I SAY DON'T LET THEM COMPETE. JUST LET THE UPPERCLASSMEN PARTICIPATE.
Who cares?
CALM DOWN.
LIKE I CARE.
C'MON. DON'T YOU THINK IT WAS A LOUSY SHOWING?
Cut it out...
HEH HEH
SO WHAT'D YOU THINK, KEIICHI?
...

I'M DISAPPOINTED THAT I WASN'T ABLE TO HEAR LEN, BUT RYOTARO'S PIANO WAS AMAZING...
HEY! I'M ASKING YOU A QUESTION!
I IMAGINED HE'D HAVE A GRUFF PERFORMANCE STYLE... BUT IT WAS SUCH A DELICATE, UNTAINTED SOUND.
IT'S HARD TO RANK THE PERFORMERS BECAUSE THE INSTRUMENTS ARE DIFFERENT... BUT THERE ARE SO MANY THINGS TO LEARN FROM EVERYONE.
KAZUKI'S DYNAMIC PERFOR-MANCES... AZUMA'S GRACE...
SHOKO SEEMED REALLY NERVOUS THIS TIME. IT'S A SHAME SHE WAS SO RIGID. SHE HAS SUCH A BEAUTIFUL SOUND...
Second Place: Kahoko Hino
Kazuki Hihara

Hey, Keiichi! Are you listening to me?
HER PERFORMANCE WAS VERY GOOD...
...BUT...
You don't hear me at all, do you?
LIBRAR
HEY, KEIICHI. WE GOT THE BOOK YOU WERE WAITING FOR... MELODIES OF THE GREATS.
It should be on the fifth shelf. Check it out.
Thank you very much...

FIFTH... FIFTH SHELF...
HUH
HUH
14
16
EISO

THAT'S RIGHT.
I DON'T UNDER-STAND.

HER PERFORMANCE WAS EXCELLENT ...
...BUT IN EVERY ELEMENT, FROM REFINED SOUND TO GRACE...
...THE OTHERS ALL OUTSHONE HER.
WHY IS IT HER MUSIC THAT I STILL HEAR?
Melodies of the Great
EXCUSE ME...
SHK
UM...
SHK
MY BOOK...
...

RYOTARO'S SO *BIG*.

HE'S GOT LONG ARMS AND BIG HANDS. IT WOULD PROBABLY BE SO EASY FOR HIM TO HOLD A CELLO...

I WISH I COULD BE LIKE THAT...
I WANT TO BE BIG, TOO.
HUH?
WAAAH
ER... SPEAKING OF THE CONTEST...
It's like talking to an alien.
...KAHOKO DID REALLY WELL, HUH?
From last place to second.
YES...
Huh?
SOME-THING THE MATTER?
OH... NO...IT'S JUST THAT KAHOKO'S SOUND IS...
HER SOUND?
YES...
YES...
Oh.
YOU MEAN HOW IT'S SO STRAIGHT-FORWARD?
NO TRICKS OR ANYTHING...
IT'S... HONEST.
THAT'S A GOOD WAY TO DESCRIBE IT.
HM...HEY!
Keiichi? Ryotaro?
Hey.
FINALLY AWAKE? KEIICHI NEEDS TO TALK TO YOU.
HUH?

And I fell asleep ...What a jerk.

IT'S NOT A PROB-LEM...

RIGHT... IT'S AN HONEST SOUND.

END OF MEASURE 21

La Corda d'Oro
MEASURE 22

School Music Com
Second Selec
First Place: Ryotaro Tsuchiura
Second Place: Kahoko Hino
Third Place
Fourth Pla
Fifth Place
Sixth Place
Seventh P
Scherzo Tarentella
"THAT'S AWESOME, KAHO! YOU'RE SECOND! SECOND!!"
"GOOD JOB, KAHOKO!"
"YOU SHOULD BE PROUD."
Daily Happenings 14
...Rubi, continued
HA HA HA HA
...it said "Nobutake Osaki."
Note: It was fixed before publication.
Well...It certainly was a wakeup call. A misread name can change things dramatically.
oh no!
It's just such an old-fashioned name!
Heh heh
Ha ha ha! What a completely different person!!
I truly found it funny.
I apologize to every Nobutake in the country...

"YOU DID BETTER THAN THE MUSIC SCHOOL STUDENTS..."
BETTER THAN EVERY-ONE, HUH?
I SHOULD'VE THOUGHT OF THIS BEFORE...
...

I HAVE NO RIGHT TO FEEL LIKE THIS...
WHAT'S WRONG, KAHOKO HINO?
EEEEK!
SLAP!
D-D-D-DON'T SCARE ME LIKE THAT!
GEEZ!
HFF
HFF
THAT'S WHAT I WAS ABOUT TO SAY!
TWITCH
TWITCH
OW!
WHAT'S WRONG? YOU'RE SECOND! SECOND! WHY THE GLOOMY FACE?
Yeesh.
YOU THINK THAT'S OKAY? ME? A GEN ED STUDENT?
Huh?
RYOTARO TSUCHIURA'S A GEN ED STUDENT, TOO. NOT TO MENTION A LAST-MINUTE ADDITION.

RYOTARO ...
...
WOW, RYOTARO.
AND YOU HADN'T EVEN PLAYED IN A WHILE!
HUH?
YOU KIDDING? I'VE ALWAYS PRACTICED EVERY DAY.
HUH?
EVERY DAY?
RYOTARO'S DIFFERENT.

HE'S NOT LIKE ME AT ALL.

I SHOULD'VE KNOWN...

...THAT I'M NOT THEIR EQUAL.

I THOUGHT I WAS DETER-MINED TO WORK THROUGH IT...EVEN WHEN I KNEW I WAS OVER-STEPPING MY BOUNDS.

GRRR

Huh?

OH...I REMEMBER YOU SAYING SOMETHING ABOUT MAIN-TENANCE...

THAT'S RIGHT. THE MAGIC DOESN'T LAST FOREVER, SO ITS EFFECT BEGINS TO WEAR OFF.

SHIIIIIIING
!
I have to replenish its magic.
all right! back in business!
...
TH... THAT'S IT?
How anti-climactic.
YEP! BUT IT SEEMS LIKE THE MAGIC'S WEARING OFF MORE QUICKLY, SO YOU'LL NEED REGULAR CHECKUPS.
WEARING OFF...
SEE YOU LATER, LILI.
Okay.
THANKS.
WELL, I'M HEADING HOME.
SURE! ♪
...
KLAK

Kahoko Hino... such a kind soul.
I'm the one who brought her into this...
Faculty
What's up with her?
She seems awfully blue...
Sigh

SHF
NEED AN ASHTRAY, MR. KANAZAWA?
Oh.
Yo.
OSAKI.
HELLO.
Oh, hey.
WHAT WERE YOU LOOKING AT?
Hm?
NOTHING...
OH, HER.

THE GIRL FROM THE COMPETITION.
WAVE WAVE
KAHOKO!!
KAZUKI.
TUP
YOU HEADING HOME?
YES. YOU TOO?
NOPE. I'M OFF TO MY ORCHESTRA CLUB PRACTICE.
ORCHESTRA CLUB?
....
Yup.
WITH THE SELECTION REHEARSALS, I HAVEN'T BEEN ABLE TO GO MUCH LATELY.
Oh.
IS IT FUN?
OF COURSE! ♪
HEY.
WHY DON'T YOU COME?
HUH?
YEAH! YOU SHOULD!
I'LL INTRODUCE YOU TO EVERYBODY!
UM...
I'M NOT IN THE MOOD...

heh
IT'D MAKE ME HAPPY IF YOU WENT!
ER...
HEH HEH ...
THERE, THERE, KAZUKI. YOU'RE MAKING HER UNCOM-FORTABLE.
Hey! AZUMA!
Perfect! YOU SHOULD COME, TOO!
HUH?
C'mon. KAHOKO WOULD FEEL BETTER WITH SOMEONE ELSE. RIGHT?
UM...
URK
I GUESS IT'S BETTER THAN BEING THE ONLY OUTSIDER...

...EVEN IF IT'S HIM.
YOU WANT ME TO COME?
ACTUALLY, WITH AZUMA THERE...
...I'LL BE TOTALLY IGNORED.
Azuma!! OMG!!!
HMMM...
C'mon, Azuma!
EVERYBODY'LL PAY ATTENTION TO HIM! Especially the girls!
Sigh
OKAY. I'LL COME ALONG.
YEAH!
Thanks Azuma!
WELL...
...AS THEY SAY, HELP THY NEIGHBOR.
RIGHT?

THREE

Keiichi is the main character in Measure 21. In my mind, I thought of him as a futon guy, rather than someone who sleeps in a bed. I also saw him as someone who's used the same desk since grade school and doesn't have a lot of swanky goods. Lots of books... but with European-style charm. (Who says "charm" anymore?) But Measure 21 had a bunch of monologues. It's hard having Keiichi talk. I heard that on the drama CDs he takes up a lot of time, even with the few lines that he has, because he says everything so slowly. (lol)

PLUS HE PLAYS THE FLUTE SO BEAUTI-FULLY...

ARE YOU KAHOKO?

IS IT TRUE THAT YOU'RE GOING OUT WITH RYOTARO?

HUH ?
Really?
IS IT TRUE?
IT'S A RUMOR.
Especi-ally after the First Selec-tion.
G...
SO WHAT'S THE DEAL?
GOING OUT?
NO WAY!!
NUH UH
N...
NO!
THEY'RE NOT LIKE THAT!
Ryotaro even said so.
SEISO

HEH
I HAVEN'T HEARD ABOUT IT, EITHER.
HMPH
BY THE WAY...
HEH
...WHERE DO YOU PRACTICE THE FLUTE? I'D LIKE TO JOIN, IF IT'S NOT TOO MUCH TROUBLE.
OOOOH
ALONE

AZUMA STOLE ALL THE LADIES.
Wow.
Well done.
I'M SORRY, KAHOKO.
OH, DON'T BE.
Don't worry about it.

EXCUSE ME, KAHOKO.
EEP
Y... YES?
What now?
Oh... SHE'S ADORABLE. She must be a first-year...
UM... I HAVE A SOLO PART IN THE NEXT FRESHMAN PERFORMANCE.
I WAS WONDERING IF I COULD GET YOUR FEEDBACK.
M... ME?
YES, PLEASE! I'M SORRY TO PUSH MYSELF ON YOU LIKE THIS, BUT I'D REALLY APPRECIATE IT!
BUT...
OH, C'MON. GO AHEAD.
?!!
Yes, sir!
THANK YOU!
Umm...
YOU GO, GIRL!
GO FOR IT!
STAND
OKAY!
BA-DMP BA-DMP
...
Oh, great...
!

WOW...
SHE'S AWESOME.
UMM...
WHAT DID YOU THINK?
IT WAS GREAT!
SMACK
thumbs up
WHO ASKED YOU?
You don't have to hit me...
Shut up!
THE MORE I PLAY... THE MORE I SEEM TO HESITATE.
I'M JUST NOT CONFIDENT...
What should I do?
EVERY-ONE...
WHAT'RE YOU TALKING ABOUT, MAI?
YOU'RE DOING GREAT.
EVERY-ONE'S WORKING SO HARD...

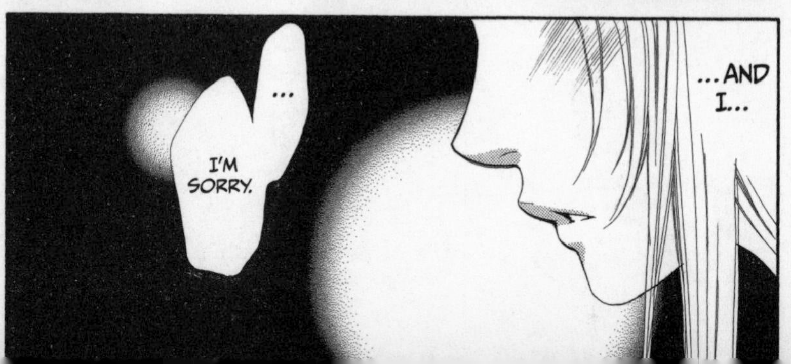
...AND I...
...
I'M SORRY.

I...
...DON'T HAVE THE RIGHT TO GIVE YOU ANY ADVICE.
I'M REALLY SORRY...

!
I'M SORRY.
Whoa.
OOPS!
I'M SORRY.

KAHOKO!
DAK
...
Hey!
OSAKI!
KAZUKI. DO YOU MIND LEADING PRACTICE?
I'll be right back.
HUH?
I WAS STUNNED...

...THAT DAY...
...WHEN I SAW LEN PLAY ON STAGE ALONE.
THE PRIDE HE HAD, STANDING ON THAT STAGE...
I COULD FEEL HIS PASSION.
HEF
...
AND LOOK AT ME.
I'VE GOT NOTHING...
MISS HINO?

I'M GLAD I CAUGHT UP.
HE'S ...
EXCUSE ME?
Oh.
I'M SORRY.
You must be surprised.
MY NAME IS SHINOBU OSAKI. I'M AN ALUMNUS OF THIS SCHOOL. I HELP OUT WITH THE ORCHESTRA CLUB.
OSAKI?
I REMEMBER HEARING...
"OSAKI, RIGHT?"
"HE'S A GRADUATE AND..."

OH!!
THE WEIRDO ORCHESTRA CLUB GUY!!
You're Kazuki's upper-classman!
※ Please refer to volume 3.
I...
I'M SORRY!
Did I just say "weirdo" out loud?
DON'T WORRY ABOUT IT.
Ha ha...
I'M SURE IT WAS MR. KANAZAWA'S DOING.
WELL... Yes.
THAT'S RIGHT. HE SAID YOU WERE A VIOLINIST AND A COMPETITOR IN THE SELECTION. AND THAT YOU ACTUALLY WON...
Sounds like something he would say.
OH... YOU'RE TOO KIND.
I SHOULDN'T EVEN BE IN THERE.
I'VE BEEN WATCHING THE COMPETITION.
I ALWAYS ENJOY YOUR PERFORMANCES.
CONGRATULATIONS ON PLACING SECOND.
WHY NOT?

...
I THINK IT'S VERY SIGNIFICANT THAT YOU'RE PARTICIPATING AS A GEN ED STUDENT.
WHAT?
BECAUSE YOU'RE COMPET-ING...
...STUDENTS WHO WERE NEVER INTERESTED IN MUSIC...
...ARE NOW INTERESTED IN THE CONTEST.
THAT'S A PRETTY AMAZING THING, DON'T YOU THINK?

GEN ED STUDENTS DIDN'T CARE AT ALL WHEN I PLAYED.
SO I THINK IT'S GREAT.
I FEEL ...
...SO RELAXED AROUND HIM.
I WONDER ...
MR. OSAKI?
YES?

...WHAT HIS VIOLIN SOUNDS LIKE.
DO YOU MIND IF I HEAR YOU PLAY?
HUH?
RIGHT NOW?
I-I'M SORRY!
It's crazy, isn't it?
WHAT THE HECK AM I SAYING?
I DON'T MIND.
HUH?
I CAN'T PLAY ANYTHING FANCY.
As long as you're okay with that.
WHAT?
ANY REQUESTS?
A-ANYTHING!
It's up to you!
THEN HOW ABOUT THE PIECE KAZUKI PLAYED IN THE SECOND SELECTION?
ON WINGS OF SONG.
IT'S A FREE, UPBEAT MELODY. I LIKE IT.
Y-YES, PLEASE!

I THINK EVERY-BODY'S EMOTIONS WAVER DURING A CONTEST.

BUT...

...THE IMPORTANT THINGS DON'T CHANGE.

I JUST WANT PEOPLE TO ENJOY IT MORE...

...THAT'S ALL.

OSAKI'S VIOLIN...

... WAS INFINITELY WARM...

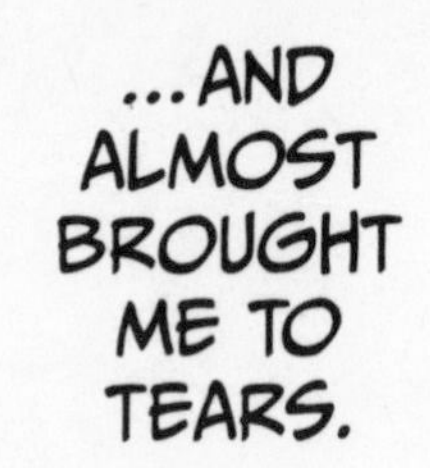

I HAVE TO APOLOGIZE TO THAT GIRL.

AT LEAST SAY SOME-THING...

SAY... "IT WAS SO BEAUTIFUL, IT BLEW ME AWAY."

AT LEAST I COULD SAY THAT.

KAHOKO!!
EVEN IF IT'S A STEP AT A TIME, I HAVE TO MOVE FORWARD.
THEN MAYBE...
...EVEN I MIGHT BE ABLE TO FIND SOME-THING...
Sorry. I was worried.
I'm sorry.
It's so like you.
END OF MEASURE 22

La Corda d'Oro
MEASURE 23

A-
AZUMA
AND...
...KAHOKO
ARE
GETTING
MARRIED!!

WAIT.
OR ARE THEY JUST ENGAGED?
HFF
HFF
HUH ?

Daily Happenings ⑮
...Smiling?
My mother's reaction to the spread for Measure 23 was...
Huh. Nobody's smiling in this one.
Check out the guy in the middle, Mom.
Please don't do this in front of me.
MOTHER
Oh, I see. He's smirking.
Azuma is a tough sell with my family. He's not smirking AT ALL. Or is he?

YOU NERVOUS?
AZUMA...

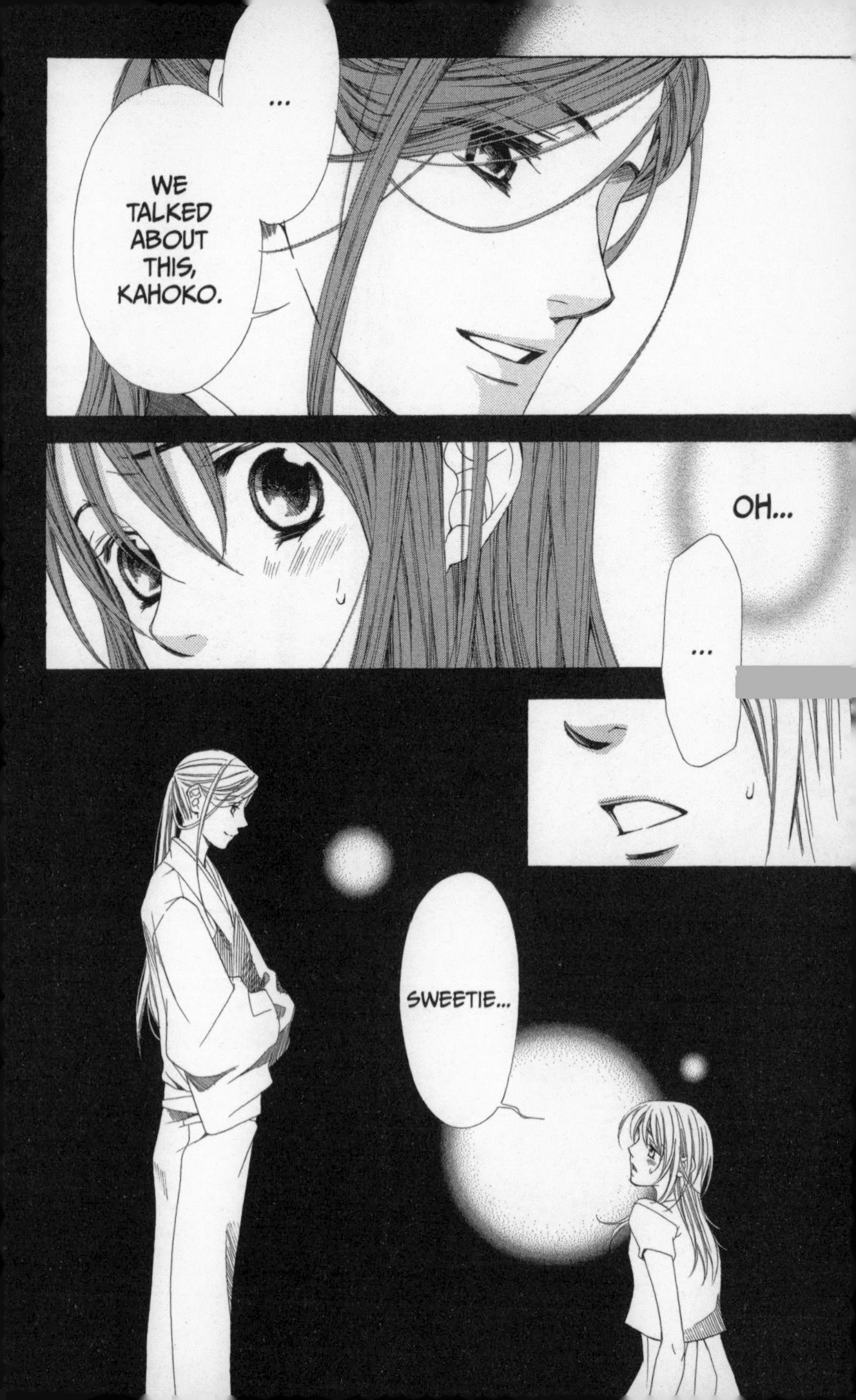
...
WE TALKED ABOUT THIS, KAHOKO.
OH...
...
SWEETIE...

Heh...
WE SHOULD WORK ON THAT.
BLUSH
I mean ...

HUH?

YEAH.
SHE'S BEEN HASSLING ME ABOUT ARRANGING A MEETING SINCE BEFORE THE SECOND SELECTION.

Uh...
WHO HAS?
AYANO.
?
WHO'S AYANO?
?
HMM... I GUESS YOU COULD CALL HER A PROSPECTIVE FIANCÉE.
PROSPECTIVE FIANCÉE?
BUT WHO DOES SHE WANT TO MEET?
SHE'S BEEN SO RELENTLESS LATELY THAT...
...I ACCIDENTALLY LET IT SLIP THAT...

...I COULDN'T MARRY HER BECAUSE THERE'S SOMEONE I CAN'T GET OUT OF MY HEAD.
THE HOUSE IS BASICALLY EMPTY TODAY. EVERYONE'S AT THE EXHIBITION.
DON'T YOU REMEMBER? "HELP THY NEIGHBOR"?

NO.
I GUESS IF WE WERE IN LOVE, IT WOULD BE...
..."BABE"?
!!
HEY.
WUP
I CAN'T BELIEVE YOU'RE BLUSHING OVER A MERE PET NAME.
"MERE"?
A *MERE* PET NAME?
HMM... INDEED.
I HAVE TO SAY, I'M DISAP-POINTED WITH MY OWN CASTING CHOICE.

IF ONLY YOU WERE...
...A HOT MODEL, OR REALLY SMART.
SOME ADDED QUALITIES WOULD HAVE BEEN MORE CONVINCING. OH, WELL...
...
SORRY TO BE SO ORDINARY.
Thanks a lot, jerk.
Heh
I DIDN'T SAY YOU WERE ORDINARY.

WHY...

...AM I HERE?
SHUT UP, LEN.
YUNOKI
Hey!
COME ON!
AREN'T YOU WONDERING WHAT'S UP?
HEY!
IT'S AZUMA.
These stairs go to the roof, right?
Guess I'll practice on the roof today.
I WONDER IF HE WAS PRACTICING UP HERE...
I should've said hi.

HEY, KAHOKO!
ENGAGED?
TODAY? SO SUDDEN...
I'M ENGAGED TO AZUMA.
TURN TO PAGE 117.
AREN'T YOU CURIOUS?
C'mon!
YEAH... I GUESS.
I see where you're coming from...
IT'S GOT NOTHING TO DO WITH ME!
NO HESITATION!

GEEZ...
OBVIOUSLY, IT *DOES*, OR YOU WOULDN'T BE HERE.
THAT'S... YOU TRICKED ME!
GRR
Don't be a sore loser.
YOU'RE BLAMING THIS ON ME?
"RIGHT...I GUESS EVERY MINUTE IS TOO PRECIOUS TO GIVE UP, HUH? YOU'RE EITHER OBSESSED OR TOTALLY INSECURE..."
WHOSE FAULT IS IT, THEN?
I should've asked Kahoko when I had the chance!
HMPH
BUT...
...WHEN THE HELL DID THOSE TWO GET SO CLOSE?
SO...
...WHAT HAPPENS NEXT?

FOUR

In the spread for Measure 22, Kazuki looks all fraught with ennui. By the way, the theme was, "some things have to change." It's one of my favorites. I've been told that it was a hit. I don't know if it had any special appeal...

And I was finally able to introduce Shinobu! I realize it was a long-awaited debut. I'm sorry.

I was planning on holding off until sometime after the Second Selection, but before I knew it I was on Volume 5...

Hey.
THERE YOU ARE.
Found you.
HEY, MIYABI.
HOME FROM SCHOOL?
IS SHE HIS SISTER?
WHO'S THIS, AZUMA?
OH...
SHE'S A SECOND-YEAR AT MY SCHOOL. MISS KAHOKO HINO.
HELLO.
Nice to meet you.
THAT'S RIGHT. KAZUKI MENTIONED HER.
Heh
"HER NAME'S MIYABI AND SHE'S SUPER CUTE. A TOTAL BEAUTY."
NICE TO MEET YOU. I'M AZUMA'S SISTER, MIYABI.

WHOA! SHE REALLY *IS* GORGEOUS!
WHAT'RE YOU BLUSHING FOR?
B-DMP
B-DMP
What's up with these siblings?
I CAN'T HELP IT, AZUMA ...
Sigh
THERE YOU GO AGAIN.
HUH?
HOW MANY TIMES DO I HAVE TO TELL YOU? I'M "SWEETIE."
HUH? OH...
OH, DEAR...
AZUMA?
HEE HEE
DON'T BE SO HARD ON HER.
I'M SORRY, MISS KAHOKO.
IT'S OKAY.
...
SO...

DID AZUMA PICK THAT OUTFIT OUT FOR YOU?
OH...
GOOD EYE, MIYABI.
I KNEW IT!
THE COLORS ARE SO *YOU*, AZUMA.
A FEW HOURS BEFORE ...
SHALL WE GET GOING, THEN?

YANK
HUH?
WAIT!
SLAM
VROOM...
WAIT A SEC!!
THAT LOOKS GREAT ON YOU.
YEAH, THE SUBTLE COLORS LOOK GOOD.
HMM... MAYBE WE SHOULD GIVE YOU A SHAWL OR SOME-THING.

AZUMA...
HOW MANY OUTFITS DO I HAVE TO TRY ON?
TURN TO THE MIRROR.
I'D LOVE TO GET YOU A NECKLACE OR BROACH AS AN ACCENT...
...BUT YOU'RE NOT USED TO ACCES-SORIZING, ARE YOU?
Hmm.
NOT AT ALL.
BETTER NOT OVERDO IT.
HERE, TRY THIS ONE ON.
WE'RE NOT DONE YET?
Oh.
WHAT-EVER WE CHOOSE, SHE'LL BE WEARING IT OUT.
MAY WE PUT HER UNIFORM IN A BAG?
Of course.
HUH?
I DON'T MIND WEARING MY UNIFORM!
Hello?
Have you seen these price tags?
YANK

I MIND.
JUST SHUT UP AND ENJOY BEING TREATED LIKE A PRINCESS.
...KO...
KAHOKO?
HUP
OH...
...
I'M SORRY. YOU WERE SAYING?
I'M SORRY YOU HAVE TO DO THIS...

HUH?
MIYABI?
I KNOW ABOUT TODAY.
I ALSO KNOW THAT...
...AZUMA'S *NOT* IN LOVE WITH ANYONE.

WHAT'RE YOU TWO UP TO?
OH, NOTHING. I CAN'T BELIEVE YOU, AZUMA!

YOU HAVEN'T EVEN SERVED MISS KAHOKO ANY TEA!
HMM? OH, RIGHT...
NOK NOK
WHAT GREAT TIMING.
SLIP
PARDON ME.
I JUST CAME TO TELL YOU.
STARTING TODAY... I MEAN JUST TODAY...
...WE'VE GOT NEW STUDENTS.

MAY I OFFER YOU A CUP OF TEA?

...AND?

And...
Umm...
We bumped into Miyabi in front of the gate...
I MEAN...
...WHAT'S GOING ON? EN-EN-EN...
...GA-GA-GA...
OH, THAT.
IT'S NOT THAT BIG A DEAL. I JUST ASKED KAHOKO FOR A FAVOR. RIGHT?
......
......
YES...
I guess.
SHOVE
GA!
KAZUKI TOLD US ABOUT AN ENGAGE-MENT.
WELL...
UNIFORMS STAND OUT HERE, SO I HAD THEM CHANGE.
They look great, don't they?

SINCE YOU'RE ALL HERE...
...WHY DON'T YOU STAY AWHILE?
SH
MIYABI, COULD YOU EXPLAIN THE DEAL?
SURE.
GOOD.
KAHOKO, MAY WE TALK IN PRIVATE?
Heh

WHAT UNEXPECTED INTERFER-ENCE.
DID YOU SAY SOME-THING TO KAZUKI?
OH, WELL.
I GUESS IT'LL WORK EVEN WITH *THOSE* FOUR AROUND.
IN ANY CASE, SHE'S COMING SOON, AND I'M COUNTING ON YOU.

...

YOU'RE NOT GOING TO BAIL OUT ON ME, ARE YOU?

LOOK, ARE YOU SURE ABOUT THIS?
TELLING LIES ABOUT BEING IN LOVE TO YOUR PROSPECTIVE FIANCÉE?
I'M SURE THIS INVOLVES MORE THAN JUST THE TWO OF YOU...
IT WON'T BE A TOTAL LIE.
HUH?
I TOLD YOU.
SHE'S A *PROSPECTIVE* FIANCÉE.
ONE OF MANY.

MY FAVORITE'S ANOTHER ONE.
SHE ALSO HAPPENS TO BE MY GRANDMOTHER'S FAVORITE, SO I'M SURE IT'LL END UP BEING HER.
AS LONG AS I LET HER KNOW SHE'S MY FAVORITE...
...I CAN PLAY DUMB ABOUT TODAY.
SHE'S THE ONE YOU'RE IN LOVE WITH?
IT'S NOT THAT SERIOUS.
I JUST THINK... IT WOULD BE THE RIGHT DECISION.
I CAN ONLY MARRY ONE GIRL, SO I MIGHT AS WELL GET RID OF THE OTHERS AS SOON AS POSSIBLE.
THE... THE "OTHERS"?
What a cad.

DON'T GET WORKED UP OVER SUCH A TRIVIAL MATTER.
TRUST ME, IT'S BETTER THIS WAY.
SHALL WE?

"BETTER THIS WAY"?
HMMM...
OH, REALLY?
...
GEEZ...
BETTER THAN WHAT?
KAHOKO.
HUH?
BEST OF LUCK...
PAT
HUH?
SHH!
SHP
EXCUSE ME.

WOW!
SHE'S A BEAUTY OF A WHOLE OTHER KIND!
AZUMA!

END OF MEASURE 23

05
HY
SU
La Corda d'Oro
SPECIAL EDITION ~Tempo Primo~

ALL RIGHT!!
AWESOME
...!
NICE ONE!

C'MON!
GIVE UP, RYOTARO!
HMPH
YOU KNOW...
...I'VE BEEN WONDERING WHY YOU BECAME A MUSIC MAJOR.
YOU SEEM LIKE A TYPICAL JOCK.
YEAH, I GET THAT A LOT. I WAS ON THE TRACK TEAM UNTIL THE SUMMER OF 7TH GRADE...
Really?
TRACK?
THAT'S FUNNY. I WAS ON THE TRACK TEAM IN MIDDLE SCHOOL, TOO.
That and soccer.
REALLY?
WHAT?
REALLY? I WAS A SPRINTER!
100 M
YOU SERIOUS? SAME HERE.
WOW...

TRACK TEAM, HUH? TAKES ME BACK...
BIP
BANG

HIHARA!
Huh?
KAZUKI HIHARA
(7TH GRADE) ~SUMMER~
WHAT'S WITH YOUR TIME THESE DAYS?
YOU'D BETTER BUCKLE DOWN AND PRACTICE! THE BIG MEET'S COMING UP RIGHT AFTER SUMMER!
What's the big joke?
GET YOURSELF IN GEAR!!
HEY!
GIVE ME FIVE 100 METER SPRINTS!!
HEY!
IT'S LUNCH! LUNCH, COACH!!
GULP
HEH HEH...
ALWAYS GETTIN' YELLED AT, KAZUKI.
THAT MEANS HE SEES SOMETHING IN YOU!
SMACK
Oww.
Dude's right.

OH, YEAH... THE MEET...
HEY...
KAZUKI...
YOUR TIMES REALLY HAVEN'T BEEN IMPROVING.
IT SUCKS THAT YOU'RE STILL FASTER THAN ANY OF US.
What a jerk.
Where're we eating?
The roof.
YOU'VE ALWAYS BEEN FAST.
YOU'RE ASKING A LOT, YU.
I LOVE RUNNING, BUT THERE'S SOME-THING ABOUT IT...
VOOP
I'M JUST NOT PUMPED ABOUT TIMES AND STUFF.
Who cares as long as you're havin fun?
Hmm...
LISTEN!
YOU'VE GOT THE TALENT TO DO WELL IN THIS MEET!
Be a little more hungry, will ya?
IT'S NOT LIKE I RUN TO WIN MEETS...

HEY, KAZUKI. LET'S EAT SOME-WHERE ELSE.
B-DMP...
B-DMP.

B-DMP
BDMP
B-DMP
AHHHH
HEY...
WHO ARE YOU?

I'M KAZUKI HIHARA! I'M IN CLASS 7-2, STUDENT NUMBER 10!
I'm on the track team!!
HEE HEE
WHAT AM I SAYING?
I...I SEE. I'M YAYOI MIYAUCHI.
I'm in the brass band.
WHOA
HEH
THIS IS A TRUMPET.
You've heard of them, right?
I WAS PLAYING "UNDER THE DOUBLE EAGLE." I'M SURE YOU'VE HEARD IT BEFORE.

I'M ACTING WEIRD...
THE NEXT DAY...
THE DAY AFTER THAT...
THE DAY AFTER THAT...
THE DAY AFTER...
...
Hey, Kazuki! See you there!
SO WHY'RE YOU ALWAYS HERE?
HEE HEE...
You planning on doing this all summer long?
Huh? Oh!
I'M SORRY!
I JUST WANTED TO HANG OUT DURING LUNCH.
I'M IN YOUR WAY, HUH?
IT'S NOT THAT...
Hee hee hee
BUMMED...
GRR
KAZUKI?

HUH?
HERE.
I BORROWED ONE FROM THE BAND ROOM.
IF YOU LIKE IT SO MUCH, GIVE IT A TRY.
Why don't you come check out the band, too?
OH, WOW...

THIS IS AWE-SOME!!
B-DMP
GO ON. TRY IT.
JUST BETWEEN YOU AND ME.
O-OKAY...
B-DMP
B-DMP

BWAAAAAAA
......
Owie!
BRR
BRR
I KNOW I'M ACTING WEIRD.
HEH. ♪
It was fun.
That felt so good.
WELL DONE.
Geez. Athlete lungs, I guess...
OOOV!
DID YOU HEAR IT?
Yeah!
Hee hee
I'M GLAD I BROUGHT IT.
OH... YOU'RE HOLDING IT WRONG.
I think.
Huh? Oh.
Like this?
MY HEART RACES EVERY TIME I TOUCH IT.

No, like this.
OH, WELL... I GUESS WEIRD IS OKAY.
BIP
SEE? I KNEW YOU COULD DO IT, KAZUKI!
HUH?
Really?
You just improved your best time by 0.4 seconds!
YEAH, KAZUKI!!
YU...
GRAB
0.4 seconds! That's awe-some!!

TWITCH
HEY!
TUP
WHAT'S UP, KAZUKI?
THE BRASS BAND!!
Huh? BRASS WHAT?
I'M SURPRISED HOW FAR THE SOUND CARRIES.
I NEVER REALLY THOUGHT ABOUT IT...
So many sounds...
KAZUKI?
HEY... DO YOU KNOW WHAT THIS MEET MEANS?
HUH?
IT'S NOT LIKE EVERY-BODY CAN GO.
YOU'RE ONE OF THE SELECT FEW, AND LOOK AT YOUR ATTITUDE!
YU?

DO ME A FAVOR AND GROW UP!!
GROW... UP...

THP

FIVE

The spread for Measure 23 is kind of like a pop star poster. (lol) A little embarrassing, but they're all trying to look the part.

This is the Yunoki edition. It's Miyabi's second appearance. As usual, it took forever to draw her. All that shiny hair... But I really like drawing her. I'll continue this in volume 6. Sorry!

I included the middle-school Kazuki story at the end. He's in 7th grade in this story. So young... But part of me feels like his personality hasn't changed at all. (lol) At least he got taller!

THIS SUCKS ...
I CAN'T FIGURE IT OUT.
Sigh...
Am I stupid or something?
Yeah, maybe ...
HEY.
IS THAT YAYOI?
SHE'S WITH SOME-ONE...
TAK
KREEK
HEY...
I WONDER WHO HE IS.
HUH?

YAYOI'S GOOD AS EVER...
...BUT SHE SOUNDS DIFFERENT TODAY.
B-DMP...
BUT...
...I REALLY...
...LIKE IT...
Hey!
HOW LONG HAVE YOU BEEN SITTING THERE, KAZUKI?
HUH?
Oh, well.
THIS IS OUR BAND LEADER, TAKAHASHI.
Hey, now.
JUST TAKAHASHI, HUH?
Nice to meet you.

I...
Hey...
KAZUKI?
Are you all right?
"IT'S NOT LIKE EVERY-BODY CAN GO..."
"LOOK AT YOUR ATTI-TUDE..."
WHAT SHOULD I DO?
DING
CAREFUL ON YOUR WAY HOME, RYO!
I KNOW, I KNOW.
Later!

This is my last column of the volume.

I never know what to say here...

Thank you so much for reading this far.

I hope you were able to enjoy Volume 5 of *La Corda*.

Lastly...
Thank you so much for all your letters. I always have a great time reading them. Thank you again.

Well, I'm looking forward to seeing you again in volume 6!

呉由姫
Yuki Kure

OMG
OMG
OMG!
THAT'S SO COOL!!
It's silver!!
SMACK
"DO ME A FAVOR AND GROW UP..."
WHY'RE YOU HESITAT-ING?

THE ANSWER IS CLEAR AS DAY.

Letter of Resignation

KAZUKI?

TELL ME WHY!!

WHAT DO YOU MEAN, YOU'RE QUITTING?
WE'VE BEEN DOING THIS SINCE GRADE SCHOOL! HOW CAN YOU GIVE UP SO EASILY?
I CAN'T GO TO THE MEET FEELING LIKE THIS.
YU... I...
...THE TRUMPET...
GO TO HELL!
YU!
YU...

I KNOW I'M BEING SELFISH ...
...BUT I...
TRACK MEET
DAMN.
!

C'MON, YU!!
Who is that guy?
WHOA
You'll be great!! Just do what you always do!!
HUH
Check this out!
WHA
GOOD LUCK, YU!!
GET DOWN FROM THERE!
CRAP!
HEY! WHAT DO YOU THINK YOU'RE DOING?
What school are you from?

Hold it right there!
I'm sorry!
ZOOOM
HIGASHI
I said hold it!!
WHAT THE HELL WERE YOU THINKING?
You trying to embarrass me?
HEY, YU! HOW'D IT GO?
I CAME IN SECOND...
THAT'S AWESOME! WOW!!
SHUT UP!
DON'T YOU THINK...
...YOU'RE GONNA MISS THIS?

YEAH.
IT'S NOT LIKE QUITTING THE TRACK TEAM MEANS...
Dude. Your best time was better than the best today.
...QUITTING RUNNING.
I still love to run.
BUT... I CAN'T GET INTO THESE MEETS.
YOU HAVE TO CONTROL YOURSELF AND CONCENTRATE ON RUNNING.
I don't hate it, but I'm not good at it.

BUT THIS IS THE EXACT OPPOSITE.
YOU CAN JUST...
...COMPLETELY RELEASE YOURSELF!
It feels so good!
I'M GONNA GET WAY BETTER AND COME CHEER YOU ON AT THE NEXT MEET!

KAZUKI!
YAYOI?
I SAID YOU COULDN'T TAKE THIS TRUMPET OUT!!
OWWWWW!
I-I-I'M SORRY!!
GRIND GRIND GRIND
Mercy. Mercy!
...
You're scaring me!
I don't pamper the kids in the band!
KAZUKI ...
OOF
Arghh...
YOU BETTER PRACTICE LIKE IT'S GOING OUT OF STYLE.

HEY, YAYOI.
DO YOU THINK I'LL BE ABLE TO PLAY LIKE THAT SOMEDAY?
LIKE WHAT?
LIKE THE WAY YOU PLAY WHEN YOU PLAY WITH TAKAHASHI.
THAT'S HOW I WANT TO PLAY.
!
THAT WAS SO AMAZING...
...
Not that you're not always amazing, of course!
SOMEDAY YOU WILL...

BOOM
Crap.
KAZUKI!!
WUP
BOING
Are you all right?
I mean, what were you doing?
Owww!
HUH?
HEE
Hey.
KAHOKO!
Oh, it's you.

SOMEDAY...
HA HA HA
ARE YOU ALL RIGHT?

...YOU'LL BE ABLE TO PLAY LIKE THAT...
Oops! I didn't mean to laugh.
I'M FINE. I'M FINE.
You sure? Your nose is pretty red...
Don't worry.
END OF TEMPO PRIMO

BACKSTAGE WITH THE JOURNALISM CLUB # 4

IT SEEMS HE COMES TO OBSERVE THE ORCHESTRA CLUB PRACTICE THREE DAYS A WEEK.
王崎　信武
SHINOBU OSAKI
THIRD YEAR COLLEGE STUDENT: VIOLIN MAJOR
BIRTHDAY: OCTOBER 17TH
ZODIAC SIGN: LIBRA
BLOOD TYPE: O
HEIGHT: 5'7"
FAMILY: PARENTS, 2 YOUNGER BROTHERS, GRANDFATHER ON FATHER'S SIDE
TALENTS: POPULAR WITH CHILDREN AND THE ELDERLY; PERFORMS AT REST HOMES
FAVORITE FOOD: PANCAKES
HE SEEMS TO BE WELL LIKED BY THE ORCHESTRA CLUB KIDS. KAZUKI'S CERTAINLY NO EXCEPTION.
But...
THIS IS A TALENT, HUH? GOING AROUND REST HOMES?
Well, I guess it's something...

I'D LIKE TO GO ON TO THE NEXT PERSON...
...BUT TODAY WE'VE GOT A SPECIAL EDITION OF THE LR PRODUCTION CONTEST!
YOU'RE PROBABLY THINKING, "WHAT IN THE WORLD IS THAT?"
What the heck is LR, you say?
YES, OF COURSE, YOU WOULDN'T KNOW.
No way.
IN THE JULY 2005 EDITION OF *LALA*, WE HAD A ***LEN AND RYOTARO PRODUCTION CONTEST!*** ACTUALLY, THE SPREAD FOR MEASURE 18 IN VOLUME 4 CAME FROM THERE. WE TOLD PEOPLE TO SEND IN THEIR IDEAS FOR PINUPS STARRING RYOTARO AND LEN.
THIS ONE.
BTW, it's a samurai theme, obviously.
Right, Kahoko?
Yeah.
That's right.
WELL, ENJOY!!

LR PRODUCTION CONTEST #1
"PLAYING WITH THE KIDS"
Everything goes here! Kids can whine, kids can cry. It's quite a sight! It'd be wishful thinking to hope that everyone gets along. But it all ends with naptime.
(Idea by YY from Hyogo; illustration by Yuki Kure)
Mr. Ryotaro
Mr. Len
THE CHILDREN'S HERO? ♥

LR PRODUCTION CONTEST #2
"TEAM LEADERS AT SPORTS DAY"
Both of them in uniform. Len has a white headband and Ryotaro has a red one. They're both living up to the part, and Len might even show off some katana skills...
(Idea by YM from Chiba; illustration by Yuki Kure)
THERE'S NO BACKING OUT!!

DUDE, THAT WOULD BE A FREAKY PRE-SCHOOL.
THANK YOU SO MUCH FOR YOUR MANY SUBMISSIONS! ♡
THERE WERE A LOT OF "SWIM-SUIT" AND "COOK-OFF" IDEAS...
...
WHAT'S WRONG?
"FROM BEHIND THE SLEEPING RYOTARO..."
GUESS WHO?
Oh, it's you, Len!
※SIR R. IS RESTING IN THE COURTYARD AT A SCHOOL FESTIVAL.

HA HA HA HA HA HA
Whoa! Could you imagine?
Yikes!
...

SPECIAL THANKS

A.Izumi
A.Kashima
M.Shiino
N.Sato
W.Hibiki
A.Shimaya
K.Hashiba
Kugaru

Y.Komuro

La Corda d'Oro End Notes

You can appreciate music just by listening to it, but knowing the story behind a piece can help enhance your enjoyment. In that spirit, here is background information about some of the topics mentioned in *La Corda d'Oro*. Enjoy!

Page 10, panel 1: Chopin's *Fantasie-Impromptu*
Fantasie-Impromptu is Chopin's most famous piano impromptu, a type of short piece designed to give the impression of improvisation.

Page 16, panel 1: Kreisler's *Joy of Love*
Fritz Kreisler (1875-1962) was one of the greatest violinists of his time. He also composed music for the violin, including the paired pieces *Liebesleid* (Sorrow of Love) and *Liebesfreud* (Joy of Love).

Page 21, panel 1: Mendelssohn's *On Wings of Song*
Mendelssohn wrote around 100 songs, or *lieder*, for voice and accompanying instrument, but *Auf Flügeln des Gesanges* (On Wings of Song) is his most famous. The words are from a poem by Heinrich Heine.

Page 25, panel 5: *Romance* by Saint-Saens
Camille Saint-Saens (1835-1921) was a composer of the Romantic period. He was a child prodigy who learned to play the piano at 2 and started composing music not long after. *Romance* is a piece for piano and French horn.

Page 29, panel 5: Saint-Saens's *The Swan*
The Swan is a movement from *The Carnival of the Animals*. The 14 movements of the suite represent a whimsical parade of animals, starting with the royal march of the lion. Although it's now Saint-Saens's most famous work, he tried to suppress it during his lifetime, apparently thinking it would damage his reputation as a serious composer. *The Swan*, the 13th movement, was the only section he published.

Page 37, panel 2: Massenet's *Meditation from Thaïs*
Thaïs, by Jules Massanet (1842-1912), is a lyric opera set in fourth-century Egypt. Thaïs, a scandalous courtesan, is converted to Christianity by her old friend Athanaël, who has become a priest. She gives up her life of physical pleasures to become a nun, but Athanaël realizes that he's fallen in love with her. *Meditation*, an interlude from the end of the opera, is a very popular performance piece.

Page 65, panel 4: *Scherzo Tarentella* by Wieniawski
The tarentella is a traditional Italian folk dance. The name comes from the town of Taranto and its local "tarantula" wolf spiders; according to folk belief, the spiders' bites either caused or could be cured by frenetic dancing. Henryk Wieniawski's *Scherzo Tarentella* is a fast, energetic piece often used to show off a violinist's technical skills.

Page 69, Author's Note: *rubi*
In written Japanese, "ruby characters," or *rubi* (also called *furigana*), are small characters sometimes written next to *kanji* characters to show how they should be pronounced. They're often used for uncommon words or names. Nowadays, many Japanese, especially young people, aren't familiar with all the words in the complex *kanji* writing system, so *rubi* notations have become increasingly common in books and manga.

Page 84, Author's Note: Nobutake Osaki
Because the way a word is written in *kanji* has no connection to the way it's pronounced, it's impossible to tell how to pronounce a word based only on its *kanji* spelling. This is often a problem with unusual or little-known names. In this case, the typesetter responsible for the *rubi* guessed wrong. Apparently, Kure thinks "Nobutake Osaki" is a pretty funny-sounding name.

Page 148: *Tempo Primo*
In musical notation, this means, "Return to original speed."

Yuki Kure made her debut in 2000 with the story *Chijo yori Eien ni* (Forever from the Earth), published in monthly *LaLa* magazine. *La Corda d' Oro* is her first manga series published. Her hobbies are watching soccer games and collecting small goodies.

LA CORDA D'ORO
Vol. 5
The Shojo Beat Manga Edition

STORY AND ART BY
YUKI KURE
ORIGINAL CONCEPT BY
RUBY PARTY

English Translation & Adaptation/Mai Ihara
Touch-up Art & Lettering/Gia Cam Luc
Design/Yukiko Whitley
Editor/Shaenon K. Garrity

Editor in Chief, Books/Alvin Lu
Editor in Chief, Magazines/Marc Weidenbaum
VP of Publishing Licensing/Rika Inouye
VP of Sales/Gonzalo Ferreyra
Sr. VP of Marketing/Liza Coppola
Publisher/Hyoe Narita

Printed in Canada

Published by VIZ Media, LLC
P.O. Box 77010
San Francisco, CA 94107

Shojo Beat Manga Edition
10 9 8 7 6 5 4 3 2 1
First printing, October 2007